Stephanie,

Thanks for everything

[signature]

CHECK THIS OUT!

Doris A. Hackett

authorHOUSE®

AuthorHouse™
1663 Liberty Drive, Suite 200
Bloomington, IN 47403
www.authorhouse.com
Phone: 1-800-839-8640

First published by AuthorHouse 1/29/2009

ISBN: 978-1-4389-1590-6 (sc)

Printed in the United States of America
Bloomington, Indiana

This book is printed on acid-free paper.

Table of Contents

Introduction

When I began this book, I initially thought to make this venture an on-going series. Please note that it was not written to in any way embarrass anyone, or make anyone feel bad about themselves. In truth, we all have our moments when we may act a little less than civil to folks. It was not intended to make John Q. Public out to be the bad guy all the time. But for now this book is from the viewpoint of the Library worker. It was written as a pat on the back to those of us in the profession of truly "serving" the public. The ones who go the extra mile when you see trouble with a capital "T", coming at you at 9:00 on a Monday morning. With the many, many attitudes and problems that come your way on a daily basis, know that you are not alone. A smile and a "Good Morning" go a long way to break up that fallow ground.

So keep smiling!

This book is dedicated to my husband Rob, and to my four children.

To Rob: You are the glue that holds this family together. I have always believed that God put you in my life for a reason. And though we may not always agree on how to raise our children, "Thank you" for hanging around to help me raise them. A real Father is very hard to find, and a real Man is even harder. I think God took out all the guesswork for me!

To my daughter Candice, who will be going to college in a few months: Make very good decisions. Because the choices you make at 18, can sometimes affect you at 41. And even if your choices end up being wrong, know that if they were made in good faith, that God will honor those decisions. And he will make "all things work together for good, to them that love the Lord."

To Tyrone: Know that if you believe, you will achieve, whatever goal you have in mind for yourself. And understand that there are many ways to get to that goal. The route that you plan may have a side road, but getting to the goal is what counts. When you make it big, just remember all the little people that helped you to get there.

To Jade: Stay happy! And realize that school is only for a season, and that more valuable lessons are learned in the school of life, than any teacher in a classroom can teach. Your favorite color is yellow. That's the color of the sun, so keep shining into all our lives.

To Tyger: You seem to know at a very early age that you will be a superstar. And you're very lucky to have a choice of what area you want to excel in. Because you seem destined to succeed at whatever you put your hand to do. Be blessed and stay humble. We probably have to work on the humbleness.

To my entire family: Everything I do, I do it for you. And though I may not say the words that often, know that "I love you." May you always remember my greeting to each of you as you come home during the day: "Oh boy, (your name here)'s home!!!"

While growing up in a small country town gave me the desire for bigger and better things, who would have thought that after moving to the "big city" I would find myself with the exciting job of being a Senior Library Clerk at my local library.

I developed a love for reading at a very early age. Not to sound corny or anything, but reading took me to places I would never be able to go otherwise. I visited foreign countries, I learned things about other cultures, and I traveled the world, through the words in those stories. I felt like I was a part of those stories until that last word on that last page. That did sound corny, but never the less it's true.

There wasn't much to do in my town. Especially since we didn't get a television until I was about eleven or twelve years old. So I used the school library extensively. When I didn't have a library book to read I would pick up old books from around the house. I ended up one day thumbing through an old medical journal from some medical institute. It became quite interesting after a while so I read the whole thing. I had such a feeling of accomplishment because it was such a thick book. I know that we don't retain even a third of all the information that we take in over the years, but I would like to think that some of that knowledge stuck with me. Every time one of my four children gets hurt playing I'm sure that somewhere in the back of my mind that medical journal info kicks in along with my mothers intuition.

I once remember being so bored that I sat down with the Bible and read it cover to cover over the course of one summer. I would set these reading goals for myself just to see if I could accomplish them. During the summer I didn't have access to our school library, and my grandmother didn't really allow me much freedom to go to the local library across town. As a matter of fact I have never been to my hometown's local library.

Grandma was very overprotective. I went to school on the bus and I came straight home. On the school bus. A few times I recall walking to town with my sister. Or attempting to walk. As soon as we got up the road a piece someone would stop to pick us and give us a ride. We would try to say "no thank you". Just having freedom for that walk to town was heaven to us. But of course there's no way to turn down that southern hospitality. "Yall get on in this car, I know your grandma and grandpa. And I don't mind at all." How to say no to a grownup in the south? You just don't.

Don't get me wrong I had some fun growing up in the south. I simply got my fun through the pages of a book. And doing my homework. I thoroughly enjoyed school. I don't know why kids today don't enjoy learning. Maybe I was just thrilled to get away from home for a while. But either way, I made the most of it.

After I graduated, I couldn't imagine myself going through four more years of school. After all, someone would get my job while I was still in college. Right? The mind of the young. I loved school and I have no doubt that I would have loved college and done well academically. But I just couldn't wait to get a job and start living. Ha-ha, the joke was on me. I need that degree. And am even now thinking about re-registering for college. My kids are seventeen, sixteen, twelve, and ten. I feel like I can squeeze it in now.

I registered a few years ago, and couldn't bring myself to go. I felt like I would have been missing something at home. Then too, if anything went wrong at home, I would feel like it was my fault because Moms are supposed to be there for their families, right? Maybe one day. I do want my Masters in Library Science. Then I could be a Librarian.

I should start by explaining that there is more to a library than you may think. There are many different departments within your local library. The place that most people are familiar with is the "check-in" and the "checkout" desk. It's actually called the Circulation Department. That's where you can either return your materials or take out materials. Hence, "check-in" or "check-out." But there's much more to your local library than just that desk.

There is also your Reference Department. Most people think that everyone who works at the library is a Librarian. Not so. That's a specialized job. And that requires a specialized degree. So when you come to the Circulation desk and ask me where a book on resumes would be found, and I point to our reference desk at the back of the room, and say sweetly as we all do, "That's something that the Librarians can help you with", don't look at me and say "Well, why can't you help me. You're not a librarian?" To which I will reply, "No I'm a Senior Clerk, but one of the librarians at the reference desk can help you." "Oh, you're just a clerk?" Pardon my slang but yall know them is fighting works, don't ya? But, I'm trying to head off an argument. I know you're tired and you don't want to walk that long mile to the reference desk. But it can't be helped. "I have to walk way back there? Don't you know where the books are? Are you new here?" First of all, that's too many questions. Secondly, I'm not going to answer all of them. And thirdly, why should I? So I reply, "No, I don't know where every book in this library is, but the librarians can look that up and point you in the right direction."

By now you realize that I have really had this conversation a few times. And those of us who work here know, that sometimes it's not even worth your effort to address all that the patrons say. If there is something you can't help someone with, just refer them to the Reference Desk. It will save you a lot of headaches. And contrary to everyone's belief, librarians don't know where every book in the library is either. That's why they have computers. They look it up.

There's also our Technical Services Department. The easiest way to explain what they do is just to say that they process all materials that the library receives, so that it is linked up to a computer record. They do much more than that but it would take too long to explain, and why do you care anyway. To make a long story short, there is a lot more going on behind the scenes at your local library, than you think there is. But, back to the main story. Working at my local library.

I imagined myself sitting at a tall circular desk reading quietly while watching over a group of studious patrons. They would come to me for advice on which book to use to find certain facts, and I would quietly but efficiently show them where to get their book. They would offer a "thank you" and a smile and go back to studying. Quietly. Imagine my surprise when that scenario didn't quite match reality. So…to help you understand the reality of a public library I invite you to "Check This Out"!

The Whistler

You encounter many personalities when dealing with the public. Your job in dealing with them is to give them the best service possible, without strangling that personality out of them. There are times when you feel like doing just that. On one such occasion a patron came up the stairs, and I noticed him right away because he was unusually tall. He seemed to be very happy also because he was whistling all the way up the stairs. I thought that was nice since most people come in grumpy. He returned some items and then browsed around for something else. When he found what he wanted, he came and laid it on the check–out counter in front of me. He was still whistling softly. I scanned his card and saw that he had a few fines. Not enough to stop him from being able to take out anything, but I thought I'd let him know so he could be aware that he needed to take care of it on his next visit. So in my most polite voice I said, "Sir, you have $1.55 fine, do you want to pay it now or take care of it on your next visit?" He proceeded to whistle and ignore me while looking up at the ceiling. So I didn't push it. It was a small fine; I just went ahead and checked out his items. I didn't take offense; I just thought he was kind of strange. Especially when I found out that he had been coming to the library for years and he would follow the same routine. I think he used the whistling as a defense so he wouldn't have to talk to anyone or acknowledge that he's even paying attention to you. Whether or not he finally paid that fine I don't know. I stopped trying to let him know anything. It was a lost cause. The more you said to him the louder he whistled! What a character. You learn to just let some things slide when dealing with these sorts of people. If it were $155, then maybe I would have pursued it. As it was, I let him stay in his happy go lucky world.

The Imposter

Coming from the south as I do, I have a rather large family. Sometimes you might have cousins and other family members that you haven't even met. However, this imposter takes the cake. I accepted the card of a young man who had several rather interesting looking oversized books to checkout. After scanning his card I thought, "Wow, he has the same first and last name as my cousins' husband!" Something prompted me to quickly switch screens and check the address also. Lo and behold the address was the same also. Now this was too much of a coincidence. So I calmly asked the gentleman in front of me, to verify his home address for me. He felt his shirt front pocket, and then he felt his back pant pocket. I told him he didn't have to give me anything with his address, just tell me what it was. He's still feeling his front shirt pocket, now his non-existent right shirt pocket, now both back pant pockets. I thought the brother was doing the Macarena; he kept criss-crossing his hands so much.

Finally, I said to him "Sir, you can stop looking. This is one of my family member's card, can I ask you how you got it?" He asked me who my family member was. I told him to tell me who it was. When he mentioned the name, I realized that he must know my cousin's husband. Apparently, he had allowed this person to use his library card. As I explained to the person in front of me, it was not permissible to use someone else's card. It may have gone unnoticed if only another clerk had helped him. But that is just another episode in the library chronicles!

I'm Broke

Our main objective is to keep patrons using the library as much as possible. So on occasion we try to be as forgiving as possible without breaking the rules. So when a patron complained that he couldn't afford to pay the late fees on his videos, I graciously cut them in half for him. After all they were $2.00 per day, per video. I don't recall the exact amount; it may have been about $20.00 all together. He said thank you and proceeded to pull out a knot of bills that could choke Donald Trump. (Exaggeration, but you get my drift) I was never so furious. I felt like I had been taken advantage of. You cry broke and then pull out a wad of bills in front of me? What could I do, I had already agreed to let him pay half, and I wasn't going to renege on my word. He paid his bill and left. The following week he returned. I purposely became very busy so that I wouldn't have to help him again. Sure enough, there he was arguing and pleading with another clerk that the bill was too much and could she please help him out. Unbelievable! Talk about cheap. After we realized his method of operation we stopped being so forgiving, but now he would argue that he wasn't told when to bring the items back so how could we fine him for it? This became part of his routine. Every time we would see him coming we would all pretend to be busy, so we wouldn't have to deal with him. Of course we all couldn't ignore him so whoever happened to be the closest to him usually ended up getting stuck with him. The things we do just to get a paycheck!

Broke, but still a Smooth Operator

I have gotten my share of smooth talkers and men leering at me from across the library floor. You have to just ignore it. After all it is a public library. It's not like you can stop anyone from coming in or say to someone, "stop looking at me!" It's a free country right? Besides they would just say, "I wasn't looking at you", which would make you look paranoid. So just ignoring it seems to be the best way to handle it. Late one afternoon as the day was winding down to an end, one of my co-workers told me I had a phone call. I figured it was my husband reminding me to bring something home. Imagine my surprise when I heard a distinct accent that sounded vaguely familiar. "Is this Doris?"

"Yes it is can I help you?"

"This is Mr. Smith (you didn't really think I would give you the name did you?) I come to the library quite often…"

"Yes, I remember you. What can I do for you?"

"I'm in Florida right now, but I will be in New York in about a week or so, and I was wondering if you would like to have a cup of coffee with me when I get back?"

There was no reason asking how he got my name, it's not good practice to become too friendly with the patrons. You never know when you might run into a wacko. He probably hung around the desk and overheard a co-worker call my name. I recognized the voice as our "I'm so broke" patron. "Sir, I don't drink coffee, so the answer is no."

"Well, you don't have to drink coffee. We can just have lunch."

"No sir, I don't think my husband would like that." There, that should end this conversation. "Do you tell your husband everything?"

This was becoming harder than I thought. "Yes I do, and I'm about to hang up the phone."

"I have a few videos, could you tell me how much I owe on them?"

"We won't know how much they are until the day you bring them back." "Well, will you be there to help me?"

"Anyone here at this desk can help you sir, if that's all, I'm going to say good-bye." What nerve! I did end up telling my husband about the conversation.

He told me to make sure I kept my eyes open, and watched the people around me. You never know when someone could turn into a stalker. The smooth operator returned many times after that, but I think he got the message. I didn't receive any more phone calls. And as much as I could without shirking my duties, I tried to allow someone else to help this patron when he came in.

Are You A Speed Reader?

Some patrons are so pleasant that we don't mind going out of our way to help them. Their requests pale in comparison to some of the things patrons think we should do for them. One of our more pleasant patrons can ask anything of me and I'll try to accommodate her. She's very soft spoken. Never screams or yells at us. She's always nice and friendly. She used to come in every Monday evening. Most times after 5:00. There would always be a smile on her face. And she would be pulling what looked to be small suitcase, the kind with the wheels and strap for pulling along behind you. When I first saw her I thought maybe she was going on a trip, and just stopped by the library to get a good book to keep her company while traveling. Imagine my surprise when she opened her suitcase. I looked down and the bag was filled with books. I thought to myself, "Well, isn't this a well read library patron?" She had all the best sellers for the week. All of Oprah's book club picks. Some I've been wanting to read. Some that you've been longing to read. She just had a lot of books! I was really impressed. When she asked me to check her record for what she still had out I discovered she had many, many, many more books at home. She had the maximum. At that time I think the maximum items allowed out was one hundred. She had all that we allowed and then some. She milled around for a while, asked a few questions about some other items. Then she checked out more books. Quite a few more. When I put her card under to check out, she had a ton of books on hold from other libraries. At least seven or eight books. I kid you not. I was still very impressed. Until that next Monday night when she came in and followed the same general pattern. Then I began to realize. This lady could not have finished reading all these books in one week. Return seven or eight, check out seven or eight. Impossible. She just liked to go home and read the inside front and back covers and pretend she read all those books. In a good week, I can finish two books at best. If they are really interesting. I imagined that she just liked to appear to be well read. Either that or she was the best speed-reader this side of Houdini.

Changing Lanes

Since beginning this book, I have switched departments in the library. You would think that would alleviate some of the "interesting" people I was so used to coming into contact with. Not so. These were just a different group of interesting people. And they had a different set of quirks. As a matter of fact I am more exposed to them now, because I have to come out more often from behind the desk to show patrons how to use the microfilm machines. I felt a bit safer when I could put out my yellow caution gate. But anyway… Check this out!

Why Shouldn't I Believe You?

I now work in our periodicals department. Dealing with magazines, newspapers, journals and such. Sounds pretty tame doesn't it? The day's newspapers are put out each morning for the public to use and then put in a holding area where we keep a weeks worth of papers for people to read. One day I glanced up at the mirror that was positioned over the back table. I noticed an elderly man with one of our newspapers spread out in front of him on the table. He took what looked like a piece of our paper and folded it up. He was in the process of putting it in his back pocket when I rounded the corner. He stopped what he was about to do, and looked up when I said, "Sir is that a piece of our newspaper?" "No!" "Well it looks like part of our paper, may I see it please?" He proceeded to pull a yellow piece of paper from his back pocket. "That's not the piece of paper I just saw you with." Yes it is. "No its not." Yes it is. "No its not." Yes it is. "No Sir, it's not. The paper I saw you with was black and white. "Well, can I make a copy of an article? "Why not, you've made copies before," I said. He took the paper he was reading and went to the copier, with me hot on his heels. As I was going through I signaled the guard to come over. I told the guard that I believed this man had a piece of our newspaper in his back pocket. The guard really didn't know what to do. (That's a whole other book) The laws are so funny these days you know. You can't touch a person; you can't accuse them outright for fear of offending them, and having them sue the library. It's ridiculous. So I left the guard to figure out what to do, and I went back to where this guy had been sitting. And what do you think I found in his seat. He had torn one side off of the pages, folded it, and I guess when I interrupted him he put it behind him in his seat instead of in his pocket like I had saw him about to do. I unfolded it and went back to the copier. The guard was still standing there in a state of stupidness, not knowing what to do. The guy has the rest of the paper spread out on the desk by the copier trying to see what page he so desperately wanted to copy all of a sudden. I said to the guard, "Problem solved, I just found the piece he tore sitting on the chair he was sitting in." Now he reversed on me. "Well," he says "the other lady at the desk said I couldn't copy anything." Was that an excuse as to why he had to steal part of our newspaper? "No, <u>she</u> didn't. There's no one here who would tell you that you couldn't make a copy. And as a matter of fact you were in here yesterday and made a copy of another newspaper." You would think the madness stopped there, but he was still trying to justify this thing. I proceeded to admonish him about how wrong it was to come to the library and deface public property, and about how all our materials were for the use of the whole community and what gave him the right to take things that were for the use of everyone. By this time the security guard had wandered off somewhere. And I do mean wandered off, because really what did I need him for? I'm the one doing all the talking and all the admonishing. Maybe he was just there to provide moral support. Anyway, I took the paper and went to my desk to piece it back together. This guy followed me, still talking all the way. "Can I finish reading the paper?" I'm taping the paper you tore and you've got the nerve to be rushing me. "Not right now, because now I have to take all the newspapers that I saw you with earlier and check through them to make sure you haven't defaced any of them also." "No, this was the only one I tore up." I blatantly ignored him while my assistant and I methodically went through each paper. We were also trying to put all the papers back in order, which was no easy task since the sections were all jumbled up. Mind you this guy had <u>all</u> the New York Times newspapers for the whole week. So we had to piece together seven newspapers, in ABC section order, while checking to see if all pages were intact. Meanwhile this guy is peeping around the corner every five seconds. After we had finished he asked to look at one of the papers. I said sure, but now you have to print your name on this card so that we will know which paper you have and so we can know who's responsible if something is wrong with the paper when we get it back. Well what do you think he told me? "You know I feel very offended that you checked every one of those papers when I told you that I had only torn one of them. I've probably been using this library longer than anyone else in this town." Like his age, and his longevity in using the library gave him justification for what he just got caught doing. With as much calmness as I could muster I replied, "At the moment I don't feel the necessity to pacify you since you're the one who has been defacing our materials. And if this ever happens again you will be barred from using the library." I have not gotten an apology for trying to steal our newspaper yet. And the guy still comes in here to this day. No shame.

A, B, G, D, E, F, T...

I always brag about the collection of materials that our library has. Chances are if you're looking for an item and you can't find it at any other library in the area, you should come to my library. We have almost anything you can think of. Even some items that I feel we shouldn't carry. I hesitate to even mention these items because when certain people hear that we carry them, then we'll have a rash of patrons asking for copies. And as it is my coworkers and I hesitate to touch the magazines after they are given back to us. Let me explain why. There are a few items that I feel are personal items and that if someone wanted these items they should subscribe to them at home. By now you may have guessed that we carry Playboy magazine. Stop, you men! Don't you run down to your local library and ask for a copy yet. Not until you finish my story. Especially if you have the same problem as our patron. You know there are times when all of us may not be too certain of how to spell a particularly difficult

Doris A. Hackett

word. But there is one patron who doesn't seem to know how to spell the most basic words. It's sad to say, but I think he asks for magazines so he can just look at the pictures. My first dealing with him was as you can imagine, pretty awkward. At least on my part. But did he care. Not one bit. He handed me a piece of paper that requested the "hold" year of Playboy for 2004. He spelled Playboy correctly. Which led me to believe he had read that word pretty often. Or at least glanced at it more than once during his "reading." I felt a bit uncomfortable. Especially after he left the area and went into our alcove by himself to "read" his materials. Then after a very brief reading time, he came back and handed me the magazines with a "thank you." I said, "You're welcome" and promptly picked up anything in the vicinity of my hands except those magazines. Thereby leaving him with no alternative but to place them on my desk and leave. Now, how to get them back in the box they came in without touching them? I know yall understand me. You wouldn't want to touch them either. But it's my job. On another occasion he came in and asked for one of last year's "Esssince" magazines.

One of my coworkers that has dealt with him also, said that she let him know that the library has a literacy program, but he didn't take her up on the offer. I guess reading is not fundamental to him. And so he is still coming to the library and asking for the "hold" year of 2004. That must have been a good year.

I've got My Eye On You

Speaking of stalkers, no library story is complete without the ultimate pervert. Every library has them. We seem to attract them like flies. As soon as you get rid of one, another one comes along. I have a tendency of giving names to some of our more memorable patrons. I try to give them famous names. But this one I just call "one eye". It may sound mean but it's simply because he has a scar over one of his eyes. Now, I know you guys are probably saying that I'm just a mean spirited person aren't you. But that's nice compared to what I should really be calling him. Now that I'm on to him, I try to make myself scarce at the desk whenever he's around. That's not always easy to do though. Sometimes I may be the only person covering the desk, so I can't leave. The first time I noticed him I was alone at the desk. Just my luck. He went into the alcove and came out with a few magazines. He sat off to the side at the first table closest to my desk. I was facing forward and my peripheral vision has always been pretty good.

Out of the corner of my eye I see him with one hand under the table and one hand turning the page of his magazine. Nothing out of the ordinary except that the hand under the table was moving back and forth at a frantic pace. At first I refused to believe what I thought I was witnessing. I looked up and turned my head toward the direction he was sitting in and the hand stopped immediately. I played it off and looked past him like I was checking out something behind him, as this was the direction that everyone entered the room from. After a few seconds I looked back down at the book I was reading. Maybe I was mistaken. But not even a minute later there it was again, that hand below the table. This went on for a couple of hours. This guy was not leaving. The hand would move, I would look his way, the hand would stop. We both knew we were watching each other. But he had one advantage. I couldn't prove what he was doing unless I jumped up, bent down and saw this fool actually doing what I thought he was doing. I really didn't want to see that yall. So I waited until one of my coworkers came to the desk. I told her what I suspected. She witnessed the hand movement, but again, we didn't see the actual act. This guy seemed to be in no hurry to leave either. He stayed for hours. I finally signaled one of the guards and asked him to come to the back

21

area. I explained the situation and asked him to keep an eye on the guy. Of course he knew the guard was watching him now, so he just sat there reading. With his hands above the table now. It was my time to leave for the day so I told my coworker goodbye and left the desk. The next day she told me the guy left the library soon after I left for the day. Our patrons have no shame. He didn't come back the next day, but he did return a few days later. And he followed the same pattern. Sat in the same chair. And proceeded to do what he does. This has been going on for a while now, and all my coworkers are aware of what's happening so we just let the guards know when he's in the area so they can come through and hang around more often during the time that he's in the library. This usually cuts down on his activity a bit. As for me, I'm not going to be the one to try and catch him in the act, things like that are disturbing to me and I'm afraid I just don't feel like dealing with them. Most women don't. So until some unfortunate patron actually catches him in the act, and hopefully screams her head off so we can ban this guy from the library, I guess we'll just keep glaring back and forth at each other. Needless to say I don't feel in any way flattered, but just disgusted. I know the situation sounds ridiculous but what are you going to do. I mean what if I just get sick and tired of the whole situation, and just blow up at this guy. Then we find out that he was just scratching, or the palm of his hand was just itching. Itching every day that he came to the library. And of course he sat in that same seat every day because the light was just better in that chair. You can't cuss the man out and risk losing your job. Or can I? Hmmmmmmmmmm………..

I Cant Hear You, Could You Shout A Little Louder

Have you ever met someone who was so nice, and so polite, but there was just one little thing about them. They were <u>LOUD!</u> My first meeting with this patron was so humorous. She was the nicest lady. As she was coming up the stairway, I made eye contact. Wrong move. I've since learned how to not actually look people in the eye. At least not the quirky people. They like to talk. And if you make eye contact they think you want to be their friend. Well here she came. I just happened to be looking her way as she cleared the top of the stairs. Now I am a southern girl by birth. So when people speak to me, I speak to them. She must have been from down home too. Cause when she noticed me looking she screeched out, "WHOO GIRL, IT IS HOT OUT THERE!" I smiled and said, "Yes mam, it certainly is hot today". When she finally got to the desk, she let out a big puff of air. I mean a BIG PUFF OF AIR! "HOLD ON A MINUTE, I GOTTA CATCH

MY BREATH." "Well, take your time". Another tolerant smile goes here. "WHERE'S MY FRIEND _____?" Before I could answer she spotted him on the other side of the desk. "HEY, _____! HOW YOU BEEN? He answered her in a normal voice. "HOW'S YOUR WIFE?"

… This conversation from across the desk lasted only for a quick minute, but the effects on our eardrums were long lasting. I checked in her items and she went around the other side of the desk to continue talking to her friend. You would think that now that she was right in front of him my ears could stop bleeding. No such luck. I heard the whole conversation. The whole library heard the conversation. I guess it could have been worse. As I mentioned she was one of our better acting patrons. Always smiling, always greeting you with a nice, loud "Good Morning!" Could you imagine that voice yelling insults, or curses at you? Let's not try to imagine that. My ears are still ringing from her last visit here two months ago.

Something Smells In Here

If there's one thing every woman likes it's a man who smells good. One day I noticed the most wonderful scent in the air. My co-worker and I commented to each other on how good the fragrance in the air was. There was no one in the area that we could see, but a few people had passed by on their way to the back tables. We figured it was someone who had passed by earlier. A little while later my co-worker had to go downstairs. I glanced up when a guy from the back table came around the corner and sat at a table directly in front of me. Pretty decent looking guy. He had a neat haircut. He was dressed well. No suit and tie, but was matching and everything. He was reading a really thick law book. I continued with my work and only glanced up again when I heard a bag rustling after a while. He was searching for something in a black plastic bag he had placed at his feet when he sat down. Well he found it. It was in a pretty green spray bottle. He began by spraying over the tops of both his sneakers.

I said on the tops of his sneakers. Not in them, across the top of them. Then he made his way up his body. He had on short sleeves so he sprayed down one arm, then switched hands and sprayed the other arm. He sat the bottle down and rubbed it in on his arms. My thoughts. "That's the fragrance that smelt so good." But now it was overpowering because it was being sprayed so close by. I thought the sneaker thing was a little strange, but he wasn't finished yet. After rubbing the cologne onto his arms, he picked the bottle up and held it directly in front of his face. I thought the man was about to spray his eyeballs. Thank God he closed his eyes at the last minute. He sprayed from one side of his forehead to the other side. And he didn't rub it in. He just let it sit there and mellow. Maybe he knew just how much to mist on because he didn't act like anything was dripping into his eyes. Now that he smelled better than good, he put his bottle back in his bag and continued to read his book. He never said a word, just read quietly for the next hour or so. When my co-worker returned, I whispered to her about his routine. As she was laughing about it, he pulled out his bag and once again followed the same routine. I kid you not. Now that's more cologne than any team of men should wear at one time. A coworker from another department came over to ask a question. Do you know that he did again? Now three of us had witnessed this. I was hoping no one else came over. Each time a different lady came over he did the same thing. Once more and we would have had a "Brut" mushroom cloud over our whole department. I think that's what it was. I kinda remember the green bottle from way back when. We were too afraid to laugh while he was there so we just held it in as best as we could. One night he sat at a table directly in front of me. I was working alone that night. Now if it's one thing you do not want to do, it's to let the crazies, I mean the patrons, know when you work alone. Because that's when they really start acting weird. Or is it just that it scares you more since you're alone. Anyway… He sits there reading a book. I was working on the computer so he was getting a good profile shot, and that was fine because now I didn't have to pretend I was too busy to talk. I know you think its presumptuous of me to think that he sat there just so that he could talk to me, but ladies you know, that we know when they're gonna try to "bust that move." So now I'm really trying to look busy just to avoid the conversation. About twenty minutes after he sat down one of our librarians walked by with a patron. He called out to the librarian, but with the fans going it was hard to hear, and so the librarian kept going. I felt an opening coming on. Sure enough…"Excuse me?" I looked over, "Yes?" "What is the librarian's name?" (Very mannerly isn't he?) "That's Mr. So and so", I said. (Name left out) "You don't know his first name?" "No, but you can ask him, he went to his desk." Of course I knew his first name, but you don't want these patrons knowing too much information. Last names are enough. He takes out a pencil and a piece of paper. "You said Mr….." "Yes, that's it." He continued to read and I continued to type on the computer screen. After a while he said, "That fan is probably not helping much is it?" "It's doing a little something." I turned back to my screen immediately. I've become a master at being too busy to socialize. He must have gotten the message because we sat in companionable silence for the rest of the evening. He kept reading, and I kept typing. At least he didn't stink….

Superstars

There are times when the day may be dragging by and you need a little levity to make the day more interesting. Toward that end, I've developed a little game that I play. It's called who can spot a star. So far we've had quite a few stars come in. Sammy Davis Jr. is one of our regulars. Shades, trench coat, even the slicked back hair. Rosa Parks comes in from time to time. The funny thing is that as soon as I saw her walking toward my desk, I noticed her resemblance to Rosa Parks. She stops in front of me and asks for a newspaper. When she goes to sign her name I almost fainted. She writes Rosa...I can't give you her last name, but it wasn't Parks. That would have been too much of a coincidence. Foxy Brown came in with a weave almost down to her feet. Busta Rhymes was here, and a man so horrible looking I had no choice but to name him Shaba Renks. I mean he was hurting. In the face area I mean. There's a gentleman now who has become one of our regulars. I believe I'll call him

Geronimo Pratt. Not because of any resemblance, but simply because of his story. Apparently, he was incarcerated for a very long time. He now uses our library to review our law book collection. We have the best law collection in the county. Besides Pace Law Library. I get the feeling he is trying to sue someone. You see he didn't do what they said he did. (Where did I hear that before?) He was wrongfully imprisoned. I learned this from one of my co-workers. I still try not to make any eye contact with him. He keeps himself dressed decently, and is polite, but you never know. When I do look his way, he'll wave and I'll say hello, but that's it. I am immediately busy again. You don't want to give people any impression that you're interested in them or their story. Otherwise, they might tell you their story. Then you'll have to pretend you actually care. Ashford and Simpson came through a few times. They had seen better days, but this couple was hanging in there together. We had to endure some of their rather loud arguments, but for the most part they still seemed "solid as a rock." Kenny Rogers came in one day. The only problem is none of my co-workers saw the resemblance because they didn't know who Kenny Rogers was. So I sang a little of the song "The Gambler" and a few people remembered what the singer looked like. I had to laugh by myself that day.

Coolio strutted in, and we all laughed at him. Hair and all. There was no mistaking him. Tupac came by, along with Ike and Tina Turner. But Ike and Tina come in all the time. And they tend to look different every time they come in. But you can definitely see the resemblance. You know them. They fuss and cuss each other out, but they're still in love.

Haven't We Met Before?

Some patrons become such regulars here that we already know what they will ask for as soon as they approach the desk. Someone may ask for the New York Times or the New York Post every day about the same time. Well, we have one patron who asks the same question every time he comes in. "May I have the numbers for the Daily News Scratch game?" So polite. "Sure, would you print your name on this card please?" He prints his name. "Thank you so much Miss…?" I was supposed to fill in the blank here. He was so nice he caught me off guard. "Mrs. Hackett", I supplied. I wasn't that much off guard. Never give your first name. "Oh, well thank you Mrs. Hackett." "You're welcome." Nothing strange there. I should interject here that this patron is also my Sammy Davis Jr. look alike. Complete with belted trench coat and shades. About a week or so later Sammy again asked for the numbers. He went and sat down, did what he had to do and came to give me back the papers. "Thank you so much Miss....?" Pregnant pause goes here. Did he actually forget my name, or was he trying to be funny. "Mrs. Hackett." "Thank you, and have a nice day."

O.K., now it's getting strange. The next time he came in, one of my co-workers was here with me. Sure enough she said he did the same thing to her. So, I guess I had to fix him. He changed his strategy this day. Maybe with two women here he got flustered. So when he said to me, "I forgot what you said your name was..." I said, "I didn't tell you what my name was." "Well, I would like to call you something..." "You can call me Miss." Stunned pause goes here. "OK, well have a good day."

"Thank you, you too." Laughs and chuckles from my co-worker and me go here as he walks away. Ridiculous. Of course he still does it. We can't break these patrons of their habits. Our patrons are like the energizer bunny. They keep coming back, and coming back, and coming back...........

Can You Read

Speaking of signs…

Have you ever noticed that people pay no attention to them? We post various signs throughout the library, notifying the public of rules and regulations, and other items of interest to them. The biggest laugh and the biggest irritation is when I see someone sitting in front of me, talking on their cell phone, while they are reading the sign that says, "NO CELL PHONES IN THE LIBRARY!" Or someone takes 3 or four newspapers to read when the sign right above the papers says. "Please take one paper at a time." Why does someone need 3 or four papers anyway? You can only read one at a time. Why not let someone else read while you're reading. Instead of having them sitting there boring a hole in you because you have all the papers piled in front of you. Most of our patrons are very outspoken though. So they will suggest to someone that it's not possible to read all those papers at one time, and explain to them how it makes more sense to let them take one of those papers. I pretty much let them solve their own dilemmas. Why get in the middle of a confrontation. Although sometimes they ask for my help. You can't not help. In which case I try to explain how the sign does say take only one paper at a time, and would they pretty please allow someone else to read one of our newspapers? Sometimes it goes smoothly. Sometimes it goes a little something like this:

"Excuse me, would you mind if someone else read this paper while you're reading that one?"

"Well, I'm about to read that one."

"But you're still reading the one you have in your hand."

"But, I'm almost done, and then I'm going to read this one."

At this point the waiting patron decides she can persuade him better than I can. And she may be right. You see she's not worrying about her job, and trying not to offend one patron while helping another.

"Look, you cannot read two papers at one time. And I DO NOT have all day. Can you read the sign? It says take one paper at a time. Now, I need to read one of these papers. Which one is it going to be?"

(I like this lady!)

"Oh, you can take this one."

"Thank You!" (Eye rolling and neck snapping comes here)

I interject a much softer, "Thank you sir." To which he nods and continues to hoard the other two papers. He must be a glutton for punishment because he knows someone else is going to come do the same thing. It's early morning. Everyone wants to read the newspaper. You might be saying to yourself, "why didn't she tell him to put all the other papers back except the one he's reading?" My answer. This guy has been here often. He's a regular. He knows the rules already. I would just be repeating myself. I would be remiss in my duties if I didn't tell him the first few times. Our patrons are very savvy though. They think they are smarter than us. The first time I asked him to take one paper at a time he pointed out that there was no one waiting to read them anyway. He was right. That particular morning it was slow. There was hardly anyone in the library. So… I'll just let my soft-spoken, sweet tempered public handle their problems amongst themselves. They get results quicker than I can.

The Abominable Snowman

We recognize that this is a public place and as such we are open to any and everybody coming into contact with us. Therefore we oftentimes find ourselves face to face with uncertain personalities. We learn to diffuse situations that some folks have to have months of training to handle. Case in point:

An elderly lady came into the library one day, and sat right in front of my desk. I noticed that she was very shabby looking. She may have been homeless, then again maybe not. She just had the look of unkemptness about her. What struck me first about her was the whiteness of her skin. Very white hands, white legs sticking out from under her housedress. (It looked like one of the housedresses my grandmother used to wear. You know the kind with all the pretty flowers that buttoned down the front). Her socks were folded down, and she had on sneakers. She had long stringy black hair right above her shoulders, with patches of gray at various spots on the roots. At least

I thought they were gray hairs until I looked closer and realized they were patches of white dirt. It was too thick to be just dandruff. Then something else struck me. This lady was black. That whiteness was ash. She was so ashy she looked like the Abominable Snowman. She was definitely the reason Johnson & Johnson created baby oil. Got the mental picture? Now it wouldn't have been so bad if she just wanted to get in out of the cold. But no, she wanted to look at some microfilm. Now there's interaction. My assistant got up to get her the film that she needed. I went back to doing what I was doing and the next thing I know I hear raised voices and I believe there was some finger pointing. My assistant was very upset. She was telling our patron how she had no right to talk to her that way, and so on, and so on. At this point I tagged in, and said "Why don't I take it from here?" So I asked my worker to go cover the desk. (Sometimes all it takes to diffuse a situation is to just excuse yourself from the area, take a breather) I began to teach the Abominable Snowman how to use the machines, while trying to stay upwind of her and also having to avoid direct contact. Once when I was showing her which button to turn she tried to pat my hand. "No, no you can't touch me" I said, while executing a perfect 3-point side step. Every once in a while during my instruction she would blurt out some obscenity, or foul words. I, of course realized that she wasn't really speaking to me. She was talking to all those little snowflakes in her abominable head. So each time she interrupted me, I would wait patiently until she finished, and then I would continue teaching her. She finally knew enough to work on her own, and so I made my way back to my desk. Sometime later she kind of wandered away from the machine. Just got up and walked away, without so much as a thank you. I don't know if she actually found what she had been looking for, or if she had really been looking for anything. She just walked away, still muttering to herself. Hopefully she left with some valuable information. At least she knows how to use our microfilm machines. After all, my training sessions make learning so easy, even a snowman can do it.

Afterthought

While working in a library may not be the picture of serenity that I thought it would be, I still manage to enjoy my job. I love to read and I have a never-ending supply of books at my disposal. If I need to do some research, I'm in the best place to be. Our libraries are powerful tools in the fight against ignorance and illiteracy, and I think people should take more advantage of them. Any kind of information you need to know can be found right here. And if by chance we don't have all the answers we can at least point you toward how to find the answers.

That's it for this installment of "Check This Out!" I'm thinking about making this an on-going story. After all libraries have a never ending supply of characters. Maybe some other library worker can continue it with their own funny stories. Every department in the library has their own cast of characters. And every library has the same cast of characters. They just go by different names.

So be mindful of how you act when you're visiting any library. We will try to be as courteous and helpful to you as we can be. You should also be as courteous and kind to us, if it takes us a while to figure out what you need when you say, "I need a book on plants." Well, John Q. Public, there are thousands of plants in the world. Catch an attitude when we ask you to be more specific, and you may find out that one of my next characters sounds a bit like you!

The State of Your Local Library

There was a time when children would only go to the library if they were forced to go. You had to beg and plead with them not to wait to do that research until the last minute. When they went, you could be assured that they were not goofing off. Thanks to that one little gray haired librarian who manned the desk. She had those thick cat-eye glasses with that long cord that hung down over her chest and behind her ears. And if you got the tiniest bit too loud she would glare at you over the top of those glasses. She wouldn't have to say a word. You knew what to do. Be quiet! People actually went to the library to do research.

Today, your local library is used for everything from a babysitting service to a youth center, to a social club. Working parents, or in some cases single parents who for some reason don't want their children in the house alone, are now telling their children to go to the library after school, until they get home from work. Should we be happy that the latchkey children are not home by themselves anymore? Or should we as library workers feel put upon because we now add babysitter to our long list of duties. We pretend that we're not really babysitting that nine or ten year old girl sitting in the corner doing her homework. But every time someone strange approaches her table, we look up and give them that look that says, "I don't know if you really know this little girl, but I am watching you, and I will remember your face." We want to kick that mischievous little boy out when he's running through the library chasing that other little guy that he just met, and made friends with. But how can you when he says that there is no one at home and he was told to stay here until he gets picked up. No matter how many times he streaks by you, you can only tell him to slow down so he doesn't get hurt or injures someone else. You wait anxiously in hopes of just seeing who comes to pick him up at closing. You say to yourself that you should talk to the parent when they arrive. You psych yourself up with anger and indignation, but when she walks in looking like she's had a hard day at work, or towing another one or two younger siblings behind her, what can you say? You don't know whether to be angry with her for encroaching on your time, or feel sorry for her that she can't afford a real sitter.

Then there's the other end of the spectrum. The parent who just doesn't know what to do with that teenager. They either can't afford any after-school activities, or they are too busy indulging their own pleasures to care what the teen is doing after school. That could be anything from finding a mate to the dreaded drug or alcohol scene. Whatever the reason, their teen has nothing to do from the hours of 2:30 until the library closes. And so now the library becomes a meeting place for all these teens that are not being monitored by their parents. We are now the stepparents and the library is now a teen center.

It doesn't help that the management has now taken up the cause of trying to bring your local library into the twenty first century technologically. We now have what is known throughout all libraries as our "Cyber Corner." Computers are crucial in this society. And so we now give access to computers to those who cannot afford to own. We even offer various levels of computer instruction classes. From your very basic beginner, to your more advanced, there is a class for everyone.

But where do we draw the line? When is there too much responsibility on the shoulders of the staff? Yes, we want people to utilize the library. No matter how young your little one is, it's never too early to introduce them to your local library. There's no place I would rather see a child, than in the library. You know there's a "but" coming right? While I can empathize with all these scenarios, keeping in mind that "There but for the grace of God, go I…" I can't help but feel a bit angry at what I consider to be an abuse of privilege. While your public library is an open domain for the public, it is not your God given right to leave your child unsupervised for an extended period of time while you go off and do what you have to do. Even if your reason is not frivolous, it's still taking advantage. It's a lot of stress on your mind and it plays havoc with your emotions to know that there are children all around you with no adult supervision throughout the day, and while you want to say it's not my problem, you as a human being can't just ignore when that child needs guidance. The public library is "heaven" to your local pedophile. They can spot a potential victim in a heartbeat. An unsupervised child is an easy target. Unless a staff member knows your entire family, it's only our judgment call that may stand between your children being abducted. We don't know if that man or woman who walks in here after your child has been here at the library by himself for two hours, is an uncle or an aunt. Bottom line, always be mindful of where you leave your child, and whom you leave them with.

Having said all that, I would just seek to remind management that we can't be all things to all people. A library is just a library. We can't become a teen center, and we can't be relegated to being babysitters. In an effort to get more people to use the library, management would like us not to throw anyone out. But is that the answer? I don't think so. People who need to use the library will use it. Those who just want to get out of the winter chill will also use it. Those who just have nothing else to do, or no place else to go will continue to use it. Not throwing someone out who is behaving wrong is not the solution. As a matter of fact that's giving all the other users of the library the wrong message. That they can behave badly and that there is no punishment. I say let the library stand on its own merit. The real users of the library who actually have a need for our services will continue to patronize their local library. Millions of people, including myself still enjoy the art of good old-fashioned reading. Or doing research the old-fashioned way, rather than surfing the World Wide Web, as everyone seems to be doing these days. I say that the library continues to be a valuable asset to every community. I would just hope that we could keep the integrity of the institution intact by letting us be a library, and not trying to make your local library into a teen center. Let your local government build the teen centers that are needed for their communities. We're letting them get away with not doing what they should for each community. And let the library staff do what we do best. So come on down to your local library so that you can "Check us out!"

Breinigsville, PA USA
15 March 2010
234152BV00001B/19/P